MW00937234

# even here, the flowers bloom

zoya aditi

1

zoya aditi

## D E D I C A T I O N

*even here, the flowers bloom. this book of
poems is dedicated to every person who
has gone through the darkest of times and
come out scarred but alive. this book is for
you. know that surviving is enough.*

zoya aditi

even here, the flowers bloom

# CHAPTERS

.

## Chapter One

even here, the flowers bloom

Poisoned Soil

i had only just
begun to bloom
and you
could not stand
to see me rise
and so
you poisoned my soil
hoping
to destroy me

even here, the flowers bloom

i never asked
for much
but you never gave me
a goddamn thing

you made me feel safe
when i felt as if
the whole world
was against me

you left me broken
and that's something
i can never forgive you for

if nothing else
at least i learned
from the mistake
of giving you a chance

the heart
cannot be trusted

how can it still love you
after everything you did to me?

even here, the flowers bloom

your words made me weak
worst of all
when you said
you never even loved me
at all

even here, the flowers bloom

never give your heart to someone
who refuses to treat it
with kindness and love

i wish that i could throw away
all those pretty little memories
we made together

part of me still thinks
the highs were worth the lows
but i know that isn't true

even here, the flowers bloom

there comes a point
where one more chance
is one too many
to give someone

i was a flower
on a peaceful meadow
undisturbed

you plucked me recklessly
from the soil
not caring if i wilted
just so you could enjoy me
for a brief period of time

even here, the flowers bloom

letting go
hurts

but it's better
to rip the band-aid off now
than to suffer
on and on

deep breath in
deep breath out

let go of him
he never deserved you
anyway

i saw the signs
before you left
i just
didn't want them
to be true

even here, the flowers bloom

find someone
who is willing
to reassure you
no matter how many times
you need it

love isn't just about
the easy times

love is about persevering
even when
it seems impossible
to keep going

even here, the flowers bloom

zoya aditi

why couldn't you have just
been honest
with me?

you wanted me for sex
you should have just said that
instead of faking so many moments
and leaving me
with deep scars
and trust issues
you selfish, selfish
piece of shit

if they don't care enough
to text you back
and reassure you
that they care

they're not worth it

i wanted it so badly
to be real love
that i looked past
the warning signs
even when
it was obvious

i am ashamed
of how easily
i let myself
be used by you

don't settle for a man
who just wants to
u s e
you

even here, the flowers bloom

a man should only dominate a woman
in the bedroom
—and only if she wants—
not in everyday life

even here, the flowers bloom

it's hard for me
to accept
that something
that felt so real
could mean so little
to you

you had the chance
to have all of me
but all you wanted
was to use
my body

and i will never
forgive you
for that

all the planets
and moons
and stars
in the cosmos
conspired
together
to bring you
and me
together
tonight

you call it 'just playing the game'
i call it
being a manipulative asshole

even though
i knew
we were destined
to crash and burn
if i had the chance
i would do it all
again

without hesitation

## Chapter Two

# The Arduous Road

life
often feels
like getting through it
is impossible

the arduous road
stretches forever
into the horizon

but hold on
you are strong enough
to face the day

even here, the flowers bloom

i wish that i
could rip out
every memory of you
from my brain

don't settle
for someone
who thinks
that waiting
for their turn
to talk
is the same
as listening

i should have known
you were trouble
by the energy
you gave off
from the very beginning

you will be the one
i believe in
for the rest
of my days

i want to write
my name
in the sands
of your mind

i will always be damaged
i will always be
somewhat broken

you accepted me
for what i am
an unfinished art piece

even here, the flowers bloom

i love the way
you capture our tiny moments
so effortlessly
so perfectly

i want to walk
through the museum
of your lifetime

be my guide
show me all
the smallest things
and the biggest moments

i want to know you
your every detail
your every aspect

even here, the flowers bloom

you make me laugh
endlessly

full of love
and joy

i wouldn't trade
our moments
for the world

you are the breath
of the universe

i hold your love
in my hands
and breathe in deeply

even here, the flowers bloom

your lips
tempt mine
in the most scandalous
of places

even here, the flowers bloom

you
were the rain
not the ominous, dark rain
but the light rain
of a summer day
bringing respite
from the overbearing heat

the neon lights
the bass of the music
your hands
on my body
and yours
on mine

pure

b l i s s

even here, the flowers bloom

the road
we travel
seems endless
and sometimes
it feels
like there is no point
to going on

even here, the flowers bloom

do not forget
that even
the longest winters
will eventually
be met with spring

why does everyone
i love
always
l e a v e ?

you give me feelings
i can't even describe

you
are as warm
as a summer day

your love
keeps me warm
through the winter

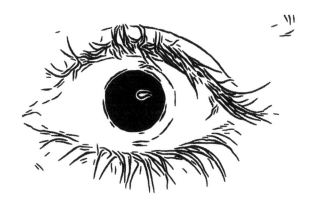

high with you
souls bared freely
i became part of you
and you part of me
we became one
if only for a few hours

at last, i understood
how it felt
to feel complete

i need you
to save me
from myself

even here, the flowers bloom

if he gets angry
when you tell him
how you feel

he doesn't care
about you

the world
seems
as if it will
soon end

so who cares
what we do
in the short time
we have here?

i love the tension
between us
as you light the lighter
and bring it close to my mouth

i only wish
that you loved me
the way
i love you

a man
who lets you
go to bed
upset

doesn't
give a fuck
about you

the storm
cannot last
forever

the waves
will one day
cease

you wiped away
my every tear

you turned my sadness
into glorious joy

## Chapter Three

even here, the flowers bloom

Mending Wounds

even in adulthood
we do not
fully understand
the depth
of our scars

i can't wait for the day
when i will finally
be free
of all
the deep traumas
left
in the bottom of my soul
by all those
who came before you

one day
i promise myself
i will
let go
of you

even here, the flowers bloom

the way
you love me

i would do
anything
for you

anything

even here, the flowers bloom

my hair
in the breeze
i felt free
standing there
at the edge
of the shore

even here, the flowers bloom

broken shards
littered on the floor
i remember you
and your anger
so many years ago

a broken mirror
a broken life
you cursed me.

even here, the flowers bloom

get high with me
let's forget our problems
and fall deeper in love
than we ever
thought possible

if you're wondering
if it's time to move on

it is.

i love the way
we laugh together
so effortlessly

you bring joy
to my days

zoya aditi

i wish i could
crack the code
of all your
inconsistent
messages

never beg someone
to be part of your life

let go of the past
throw it
to the wind

you are free.

you held
my hand in yours
—nothing ever felt
so perfect.

life is too short
to not tell
the people you
love

how much
you care about them

even here, the flowers bloom

let me touch your soul
even a little bit
with my words

you
are my anchor
keeping me
safe
from the storm

don't settle
for people
who are willing
to have
one-sided
relationships

it's okay to hold back
and retreat into your shell
when you need to

sometimes
you just need
to focus on yourself
block out the world
and fight for your peace

loving you
was like
floating
in outer space

in some ways beautiful
in some ways free
but also
cold
and distant

even here, the flowers bloom

i wish i wasn't
so anxious
to make
the same mistakes
over and over again

you can overcome
anything
in your life
as long
as you remember
who you are

you have a power
deep within you
that can change
the world

as long
as your heart
still beats
you have the fire
that can change
the world

# Chapter Four

## The Flowers Bloom

don't fall in love
with people
who are still in love
with someone else

the flower blooms
effortlessly
without a thought or care

you
can do the same
if only
you learn
to let go

i can't wait for the day
where i finally
feel free

free to smile
free to move on
free to celebrate
free to change

free

as long
as you have
yourself

you have
everything
you need

i believe
it was important
for me
to live through
loving you
so i could learn
how
it's not supposed to feel
when someone
'loves'
you

even here, the flowers bloom

the light
will lead you
where you need to go

i would rather be alone
than be loved by a man
who doesn't
actually
truly
care about me

do not settle
for someone
who would not
go
to the ends
of the earth
for you

there is nothing more powerful
than a woman
who finally
understands
just how much
she is worth

even here, the flowers bloom

city lights
masquerading as stars

just as you
masqueraded
as someone
who loves me

the past
should not
define
who you are

what really defines you
is this exact moment
where everything comes together
and you learn
exactly who
you are meant to be

you told me you loved me
and then left
as if those
aren't two
distinctly opposite
things

i wish that we
could have changed
the curves
and bends
of our lonely road

the one you want
right now
isn't always
the one
you are meant
to be with

i think
that the world would be better
if men
didn't shy away
from the word
'beautiful'

you aren't always ready
for life
to throw you off balance

but you will come
to appreciate
how much you need it
after it happens

i know i will never forget you
or what we had together

i woke up today
for the first time
in a long time
not feeling
the weight
and devastation
of your absence

finally
i feel
like there is hope
that one day
i will again
feel
whole

do not be
so concerned
with all these little things
that cause
your heart
to worry

set your soul free
weightless
and find
your
peace

even here, the flowers bloom

i want to watch you
become
the ultimate
version
of who you can be

even here, the flowers bloom

remember why you are doing this

remember why
you are searching
for love

remember that
it is all leading
to something perfect
something whole
something beautiful

even here, the flowers bloom

i have finally buried
my love for you
it took everything
i had
but i finally fucking did it

even here, the flowers bloom

as soon as you begin
to feel whole
know that he
will come crawling back
wanting to break you
again

be strong
do not give him
the time of day
or night

i will wear
the scars you gave me
with pride

not because
it has anything to do
with you

but because
each scar
represents
a way
i overcame
the ways
you hurt me

i am free
despite
everything
that has happened
to me

even here
life goes on

even here
the flowers bloom

even here, the flowers bloom

zoya aditi

Even Here, The Flowers Bloom is a
poetry book about recovering from
deep traumas, leaving an abusive
relationship, and finding healing from
all the ways you've been hurt before.

thank you for reading.

Made in the USA
San Bernardino,
CA